The Prodigal Journey: Lessons of Grace, Mercy and Redemption

By Dr.Gima Mathew

Table of Contents

Dedication.. i

About the Author ii

CHAPTER 1: Setting the Stage: Understanding the Journey of Grace 2

CHAPTER 2: Lost and Found: The Prodigal Son...6

CHAPTER 3: A Heart Revealed: The Older Brother 10

CHAPTER 4: The Embrace of Grace: The Father 14

CHAPTER 5: Living the Lessons: Wisdom for Our Lives 20

    1.   The Younger Son 21

    2.   The Older Son...21

    3.   The Father's Heart 22

Summary...23

References...24

Dedication

Dedicated to the Almighty God.

About the Author

Dr. Gima is an Engineer by profession with a deep passion for exploring the spiritual wisdom of the bible. Inspired by the timeless relevance of biblical parables, Gima seeks to uncover lessons of grace, mercy, and redemption that can transform our daily lives and inspire purposeful living. Lessons of Grace, Mercy and Redemption is her debut book, born from a desire to share these.

Credit: https://www.freebibleimages.org

CHAPTER 1:
Setting the Stage: Understanding the Journey of Grace

The Parable of the Prodigal Son is one of the most famous parables of Jesus in the New Testament of the Bible. This parable is also known by different names, such as "The Lost Son" and "The Loving Father," which depict the nature of the main characters in the story.

This very touching and best-remembered parable appears in the Gospel of Luke 15:11-32, where Jesus shares this parable with his disciples, the Pharisees and others. Although this is an imaginary story, we can point out that this parable is to teach the depth of God's love for each one of his children, even when we are sinners.

The background of a biblical passage often helps us to better understand its meaning. The scene behind this parable can be found in the gospel of Luke 15:1-2, where it says that the Pharisees and scribes deride Jesus for welcoming sinners and dining with them. This implies that the Pharisees, who were the Jewish religious leaders at that time, it was inappropriate for a 'godly person' to interact with sinners. This criticism sets the stage for three parables (the third being the Prodigal Son) in which Jesus challenges their assumptions and reveals how God the Father lovingly embraces sinners.

Credit: https://www.freebibleimages.org

The first parable is about a lost sheep from the flock of ninety-nine (Luke 15:4-7), the second is about a lost coin (Luke 15:8-10), and the third is about the Prodigal Son (Luke 15:11-32). The three parables reinforce one key idea, showing Jesus's character as a great teacher. The same morale was conveyed to different people in that society through three different stories. The Lost Sheep parable might appeal to shepherds (perhaps representing the working class) because of their personal connection to the flock, as they understand it better. The lost coin would resonate with the poor because of its immediate value, and the prodigal son would speak to the wealthy or landlords because of the inheritance and family dynamics at stake. By using three different illustrations, Jesus conveys the same truth. No matter who you are, the loss of something valuable is deeply painful, but the joy of finding it is immeasurable.

This parable of the Prodigal Son appears only in Luke's Gospel (Luke 15:11-32). In this parable, the focus is primarily on the father and his two sons. The younger son asks for his share of the inheritance, leaves home, and squanders his wealth in reckless living. When a famine strikes, he is left destitute and forced to work as a swineherd—an act considered particularly degrading to Jewish people, as pigs were considered unclean animals. Eventually, he comes to his senses and decides to return to his father, hoping to be accepted back as a servant. But instead of rebuke, the father welcomes him with open arms, throwing a feast in his honour. This unexpected love causes the elder son to become jealous and resentful.

Although we are deeply touched by this story of the love of the father towards a reckless son, the other characters in the story also teach us valuable lessons.

In the 'Prodigal Son', we find four significant characters: the prodigal son, the father, the elder son, and God. As we examine these characters more closely in the chapters that follow, we will explore the deeper meanings of their actions and what they can teach us about forgiveness, grace, and our relationship with God. Let us explore what lessons this parable teaches and how they can inspire our own lives.

Credit: https://www.freebibleimages.org

CHAPTER 2:
Lost and Found: The Prodigal Son

As the name of the parable suggests, the second son of the man is the prodigal son. The general thought about the man's second son, who demanded his share from the father rather than waiting for his father's death, is that he was unfaithful, disobedient, and selfish.

Credit: https://www.freebibleimages.org

Jesus continued: *"There was a man who had two sons. The younger one said to his father, 'Father, give me my share of the estate.' So, he divided his property between them. Not long after that, the younger son got together all he had, set off for a distant country, and there squandered his wealth in wild living."* (Luke 15:11-13)

As human beings, we find several reasons to think of him as a prodigal son. The first thing that may come to our mind is that, despite being under his father's blessings and having everything he needed, he did not realise it. The second is that he could have stayed home and supported and helped his father and would have had a great life with his family.

The thought that made him leave his father may have been his belief that he would do well on his own, as he was old enough to care for himself and build a better life than the one he had with his father and family. However, he soon realises the truth in a hard way. His actions did not lead him to success.

"When he came to his senses, he said, 'How many of my father's hired servants have food to spare, and here I am starving to death! I will set out and go back to my father and say to him: Father, I have sinned against heaven and against you. I am no longer worthy to be called your son; make me like one of your hired servants.' So he got up and went to his father." (Luke 15:17-20)

Credit: https://www.freebibleimages.org

Although the son thought that his father and other family members would not be happy with his behaviour, he was still willing to try and return home. He even planned how he would approach his return. He rehearsed his speech in which he humbly admitted his sin against the Father in heaven, declaring himself unworthy. He intended to ask his father to accept him as a servant to atone for his behaviour. At that time, he did not consider how the rest of the family might receive him.

When he realised he couldn't manage on his own without his father; he chose to seek his father's forgiveness. He could have let his ego take over and continue down a path of destruction, but instead, he showed humility by asking for forgiveness from his father. Similarly, in our own lives, we may act against the will of our Father in heaven, just as we sometimes go against the will of our earthly parents. Yet, if we acknowledge our mistakes, humble ourselves, and seek forgiveness without pride, we will find that our heavenly Father is loving and compassionate.

Credit: https://www.freebibleimages.org

CHAPTER 3:
A Heart Revealed: The Older Brother

While the Parable of the Prodigal Son often focuses on the younger son's rebellion and repentance, Jesus masterfully highlights another crucial figure: the older brother.

The *Scripture says:*

"Meanwhile, the older son was in the field. When he came near the house, he heard music and dancing. So, he called one of the servants and asked him what was going on. 'Your brother has come,' he replied, 'and your father has killed the fattened calf because he has him back safe and sound.' (Luke 15:25-27)

The older brother's reaction was immediate:

"The older brother became angry and refused to go in. So, his father went out and pleaded with him. But he answered his father, 'Look! All these years, I've been slaving for you and never disobeyed your orders. Yet you never gave me even a young goat so I could celebrate with my friends. But when this son of yours who has squandered your property with prostitutes comes home, you kill the fattened calf for him!" (Luke 15:28-30).

The older brother is often seen as the "obedient" son—the one who stayed, worked hard, and followed his father's orders. Yet beneath this veneer of loyalty lies a heart filled with bitterness, self-righteousness, and jealousy. He feels betrayed by his father's lavish celebration for the prodigal son and struggles to understand the depth of his father's love and forgiveness.

The older brother's grievances reveal much about his heart. Though he stayed in the house, his heart was far from his father's. He harboured a sense of entitlement, assuming that his loyalty guaranteed him a superior place in his father's affections. His words suggest that he views his relationship with his father as transactional: "I've been slaving for you," he says, reducing his years of service to mere duty rather than an expression of love or familial bond. He measures his worth by his work and obedience, failing to recognise that his father's love is not something to be earned but freely given. In this way, he was as lost as the younger son—just in a different way.

While the prodigal son's sins were visible, the older brother's sins of pride, resentment, and self-righteousness remained hidden. Through him, we see that the father has, in a way, lost both sons—one physically and the other emotionally. Though physically present, the older brother harbors resentment, pride, and misunderstanding. Jesus reveals that both sons need to experience repentance and transformation.

Credit: https://www.freebibleimages.org

CHAPTER 4:
The Embrace of Grace: The Father

The Parable of the Prodigal Son, though an imaginary story, vividly illustrates the profound and boundless love of God the Father for all of us. Even in our moments of sinfulness and recklessness, God's love remains steadfast, longing for our return. Through this story, Jesus reveals His mission to save all people, including those often deemed outcasts—"tax collectors and sinners."

Jesus narrates:

"But while he was still a long way off, his father saw him and was filled with compassion for him; he ran to his son, threw his arms around him and kissed him." (Luke 15:20)

This moment is central to understanding the father's heart. The father was not merely resigned to his son's departure but was filled with hope, watching and waiting for his return. The act of running toward the son, a gesture of undignified urgency in that culture, demonstrates the father's overwhelming love and eagerness to reconcile.

"The son said to him, 'Father, I have sinned against heaven and against you. I am no longer worthy to be called your son.'" (Luke 15:21)

Before the son could even complete his rehearsed confession, the father embraced him, showing that his love transcended words or conditions. There was no lecture, condemnation, or mention of past mistakes. Instead, there was pure, unreserved acceptance.

The father's response is extraordinary:

"But the father said to his servants, 'Quick! Bring the best robe and put it on him. Put a ring on his finger and sandals on his feet. Bring the fattened calf and kill it. Let's have a feast and celebrate. For this son of mine was dead and is alive again; he was lost and is found.' So they began to celebrate." (Luke 15:22-24)

This act of restoration is rich with symbolism. The best robe signifies honour, the ring represents authority and family identity, and the sandals mark his restored status as a free man—not a servant. The father not only forgave his son but also celebrated his homecoming with a feast. His joy was uncontrolled; it was extravagant and inclusive, inviting everyone to share in the celebration.

This parable reflects a father who is far from ordinary. He did not chastise his son for leaving or lecture him on his failures. Instead, he respected his son's free will, even when it led to poor choices. He divided his property without protest and allowed his son to embark on a journey of self-discovery. While the father likely experienced pain and sorrow, he trusted that life itself would teach his son valuable lessons.

What is most striking about this father is his unwavering hope and readiness to forgive. He did not keep the score of his son's wrongdoings, nor did he compare him to his obedient older brother. Instead, his heart was filled with mercy, a mercy that reflects the very nature of God.

Credit: https://www.freebibleimages.org

Jesus also shows compassion and mercy towards his older son.

"'My son', the father said, 'you are always with me, and everything I have is yours'" (Luke 15:31).

The father calls him "My Son" showing his tenderness and reaffirming that he is not forgotten and entitled to his full inheritance despite his pride and resentment.

For us, the father in this parable is a reminder of God's infinite grace. Even when we stray, make mistakes, or feel unworthy, God eagerly waits for our return, ready to restore us as His beloved sons and daughters. In His mercy, we find freedom, redemption, and the hope of a fresh start.

The Parable of the Prodigal Son is not just a tale of a father and his wayward son; it is an invitation to understand the vastness of God's love—a love that is always seeking, always forgiving, and always ready to celebrate our return.

CHAPTER 5:
Living the Lessons: Wisdom for Our Lives

The story of the prodigal son challenges us to reflect on our own lives and choices. It highlights the classic human tendency to sacrifice what is truly valuable for fleeting desires.

In many ways, this parable mirrors our own spiritual journey. Life is a continuous process of returning to the Father's house, fuelled by a desire to change and a commitment to self-improvement. However, such transformation often requires sacrifice—letting go of pride, sinful habits, or destructive choices.

Only when the younger son has wasted his inheritance and finds himself destitute does he begin to see the truth. Reduced to feeding swine—an animal considered unclean in Jewish culture—and longing to eat the pigs' food, he experiences a moment of clarity. His desperate state forces him to remember the abundance and care he once enjoyed in his father's house. This realisation sparks a longing for home and sets the stage for his transformation.

Wisdom for Our Lives

The parable carries profound lessons for us:

1. The Younger Son

The younger son represents those who stray from God, pursuing worldly pleasures or selfish desires. His journey reminds us of the emptiness of a life lived apart from God's presence. His journey back home, marked by repentance, reflects God's boundless mercy and His readiness to forgive those who return with a sincere heart. The father's embrace is a powerful reminder that no matter how far we fall, God's love is always waiting to restore us. It also teaches us that God's mercy is always greater than our sin, no matter how far we wander.

Through the younger son, Jesus calls us to recognise the importance of repentance and humility. Do we acknowledge our shortcomings and return to God, or do we continue in our own ways? The story reminds us that God's grace is not based on our past actions but on His endless love for us. It challenges us to leave behind the shame of our mistakes, humble ourselves, and trust in the Father's forgiveness, knowing that we are always welcomed home in His arms.

2. The Older Son

The older son represents those who are outwardly obedient but inwardly self-righteous. His resentment toward his brother reveals a lack of understanding of his father's grace. This reminds us that faith is not about earning God's love through works but about embracing His unconditional grace and extending it to others.

Through the older brother, Jesus teaches us to examine our hearts. Are we serving God out of love or duty? Do we harbor resentment when others receive blessings? The older brother's story challenges us to let go of pride, embrace humility, and celebrate with the Father when the lost are found.

3. The Father's Heart

The father's character remains constant throughout the story—a picture of God's boundless love. He rejoices not in punishment but in restoration, welcoming the repentant son with open arms and lavishing him with forgiveness. The father's compassion overshadows the son's sinfulness, demonstrating that God's goodness is what draws us to repentance.

Unlike the shepherd searching for the lost sheep or the woman diligently seeking the lost coin in the preceding parables, the father does not actively pursue his son. Instead, he respects his son's free will, allowing him to make his own choices and experience their consequences. Yet the father waits patiently, with an open heart and arms ready to embrace his son upon his return.

The shift in the narrative—from the search for one among a hundred (the lost sheep) to one among ten (the lost coin) to one of two sons—highlights the increasingly personal nature of God's love. The progression emphasises how deeply God cares for each individual and the personal attention He gives to every soul.

Summary

As we come to the end of this journey through the Parable of the Prodigal Son, we are reminded of the infinite love and mercy that our Heavenly Father has for each one of us. No matter how far we stray or how deeply we may fall, His arms are always open, waiting to embrace us with grace, forgiveness, and unconditional love.

Both sons were lost in their own ways, and both required the father's love to be made whole. As readers, we are invited to see ourselves in both brothers—the rebellious prodigal and the resentful elder—and to find hope in the unwavering love and mercy of the Father, who seeks reconciliation with all His children.

This story also challenges us to embrace the same mercy in our relationships. How often do we hold grudges or struggle to forgive? The father's example calls us to love unconditionally, to welcome others back without hesitation, and to celebrate restoration rather than dwell on past wrongs.

Like the father in the parable, God does not keep count of our wrongs or hold our past against us. He rejoices in our return, no matter how many times we wander. So, let us take heart, knowing that we are never beyond the reach of His love. Our mistakes do not define us; His mercy does. And when we, like the prodigal son, turn back toward Him, we find not condemnation but a feast of grace, a celebration of restoration, and the unshakable promise that we are forever His beloved children. Jesus also extends his patience, mercy and reassurance to those trapped in pride and self-righteousness like the older brother. May this truth move us to live with humility, forgiveness, and a renewed sense of gratitude for the Father who always welcomes us home.

References

1. The Holy Bible, New International Version. (2011). Zondervan.

2. Free Bible Images. (n.d.). *Prodigal Son*. Free Bible Images. https://www.freebibleimages.org/photos/prodigal-son/

www.ingramcontent.com/pod-product-compliance
Lightning Source LLC
Chambersburg PA
CBHW042240140626
46547CB00036B/100